THE CHOCOLATE WEDDING

FOR STEPHEN

also by Posy Simmonds

FRED

LULU AND THE FLYING BABIES

This is a Borzoi Book published by Alfred A. Knopf, Inc.

Copyright © 1990 by Posy Simmonds
All rights reserved under International and Pan-American Copyright Conventions. Published in the
United States by Alfred A. Knopf, Inc., New York. Distributed by Random House, Inc., New York. Originally
published in Great Britain by Jonathan Cape Limited, London, in 1990.
First American Edition, 1991   Manufactured in Italy   1 2 3 4 5 6 7 8 9 10

Library of Congress Cataloging-in-Publication Data
Simmonds, Posy. The chocolate wedding / Posy Simmonds.—1st American ed.   p.   cm.
Summary: An overindulgence in chocolate the night before her aunt's wedding causes Lulu to have
some very strange dreams.
ISBN 0-679-81447-7 (trade)   ISBN 0-679-91447-1 (lib. bdg.)
[1. Dreams—Fiction. 2. Weddings—Fiction. 3. Cartoons and comics.]   I. Title.   PZ7.S5913Ch   1991
[E]—dc20   90-4932   CIP   AC

THE CHOCOLATE WEDDING

POSY SIMMONDS

Alfred A. Knopf   New York

Lulu is going to be a bridesmaid in a silvery pink dress....

Her Aunt Carrie is going to be a br in a long white one. *Everyone* a Lulu's school knows this.

It sticks out to HERE, my aunty's dress does...

It's got **TWO HUNDRED** petticoats!

TWO HUNDRED!?

Yes! And it cost a MILLION dollars!

A MILLION?

Yes!

It's got **DIAMONDS** all over it

REAL ones

Yes! And she's going to the church in a **SILVER** carriage!

REAL silver?

yes!

And **I'm** the one who holds her train!

A REAL train?

Naoh! Sshjoopi

Not a **REAL** train! It the traily bit behind her skirt.....

Lulu will be staying at her grandparents' house for the wedding....

On the evening before the wedding, Lulu, her mother and father and her little brother, Willy, drive to Granny and Grandpa's house........

All the grown-ups are busy moving furniture and preparing food for the wedding party.....

Lulu and Willy go in the dining room. The wedding cake sits on a table covered in a long, white cloth. It looks much smaller today....not nearly as big as Mrs Clarke.

Cake!

Lulu hides in a corner, near the radiator.

Inside her case are all the things she and Willy have been given for Easter: chocolate eggs, chocolate money, six chocolate soldiers and six chocolate kittens.....

Lulu eats three chocolate kittens and sixteen eggs.

Some of the eggs have insides she doesn't like.

Eeuch!

She spits these out. and hides them und the radiator.

yuk

Lulu always puts things she doesn't like behind radiators. There's already a bit of beetroot from supper...and a biscuit she got tired of.

Cake!

Man!

Lady!

Willy?   What you doing?

No!

Will-ee?

What you eating? ...Show me!

No!

Elaahh!   Owh, NO!

here's the ride? Oh **NO!**

Mummee! Willy's eaten the *bride!*

Tsk!

Oh no! Look what he's done!

Naughty boy! very naughty!

And **YOU**, Lulu! What's that round your mouth? **CHOCOLATE!**

Right... Come on..

Time for **BED!**

here aren't enough beds for everyone at Granny's ouse. Lulu is sleeping on the sofa.....

Now, off to sleep, Lulu...

It's a big day tomorrow...

Sweet dreams!

It's the next day and everyone is ready to go to the church for the wedding, except Lulu. She was very sick in the night. She still feels ill.....

I wanted to be a **bridesmaid**....

But I don't think you're well enough to go to the church, darling...

Have a little rest now, ...then you'll feel better for the party, later....

You keep nice and warm...and we'll be back very soon

Jenny from next door...

...and the ladies doing the waitressing will all keep an eye on you.

lu watches Aunt Carrie get into the wedding r. It's not a silver carriage. It's Grandpa's r, with white ribbons on it.

SNIFF!

There, Lulu...have a little snooze.....

BOO-HOO!

BOOo-HOOo!

?

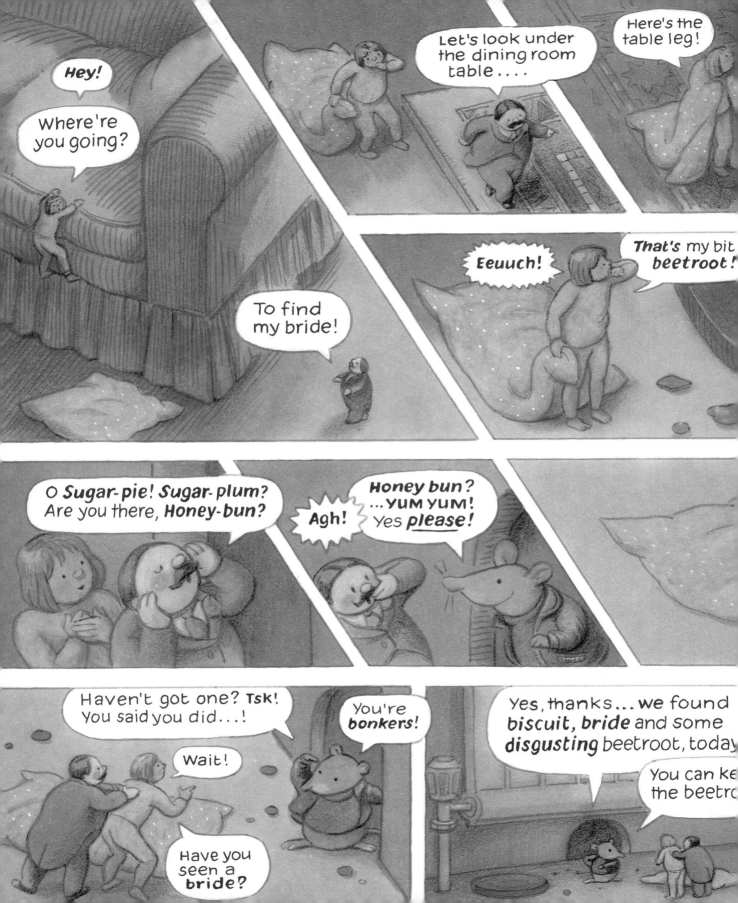

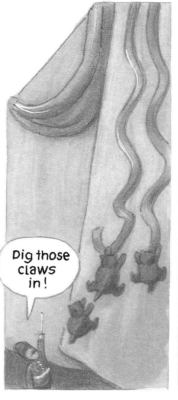

Oh!

Feeling better, Lulu?

Mum, I just fell off the top of the wedding cake....!

DID you?

Let's wash..and put your dress on shall we?

Mum!

I dreamt I found the **Sugar bride!**

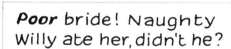

Poor bride! Naughty Willy ate her, didn't he?

No, he didn't!

I dreamt he threw her on the floor!

P'raps he did ...let's go and see.

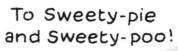

To Sweety-pie
and Sweety-poo!